How to Draw

Nativity

Step-by-step with

Steve Smallman

CANDLE BOOKS

BEFORE WE BEGIN...

Here are some drawing tips to help you!

1 DON'T PANIC!

Drawing is fun! If you worry too much about 'doing it wrong' you probably will! Enjoy yourself! Press lightly to start with so you can rub out your construction lines and 'mistakes' at the end.

2 FACES!

Here are a few simple tips to help you to draw faces. Start with an egg shape:

A

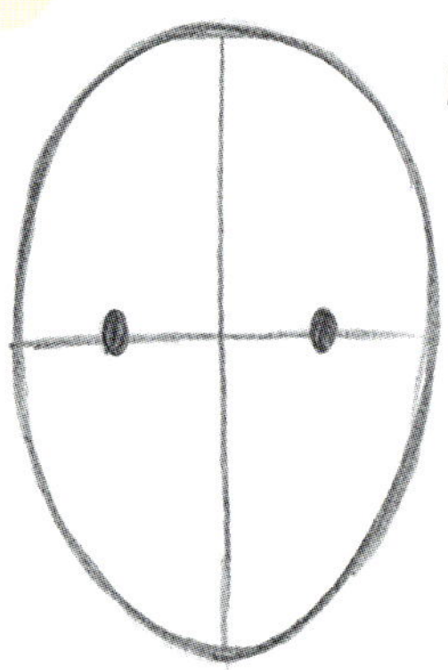

Draw a line halfway down and another halfway across. (This is for the eyes!)

B

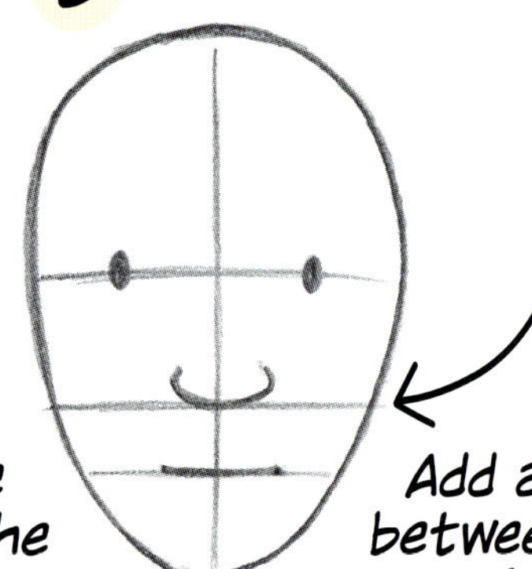

Draw another line halfway between the 'eyeline' and the chin.

The nose goes here.

Add another line halfway between the nose and chin. (That's where the mouth goes!)

C

Add hair.

Add eyebrows.

Add ears level with eyes.

Add lines for lips.

3 HANDS!

Start with a rectangle:

Add a thumb. Add fingers.

Fold bottom three fingers in to point.

Fold thumb down and fold all the fingers to make a fist.

Fan fingers out to wave.

4 FACIAL EXPRESSIONS

Changing the mouth and eyebrows can totally alter the expression of your face drawing!

HAPPY

Draw high eyebrows and a big smile!

SAD

Draw eyebrows like the sides of a volcano!

Add a down-turned mouth.

Add tears.

CONFUSED!

Draw one eyebrow going down, one going up, and the mouth doing both!

GRUMPY!

Add inward sloping eyebrows!

Draw a downturned mouth.

ANGRY!

Draw very steep, sloping eyebrows.

The mouth is like a bent fishfinger!

SHOCKED!

Draw very high eyebrows.

Add wide eyes.

Add a small, round mouth.

These expressions work on animals too!

5 SHADING AND SHADOWS!

Decide where the light is coming from and shade on the opposite side.

And if you use paint to colour your drawings...

Wash your brush between colours (or everything will get muddy)!

MARY

This special young lady was the mother of Jesus.

1

Start with an oval and a bendy rectangle.

2

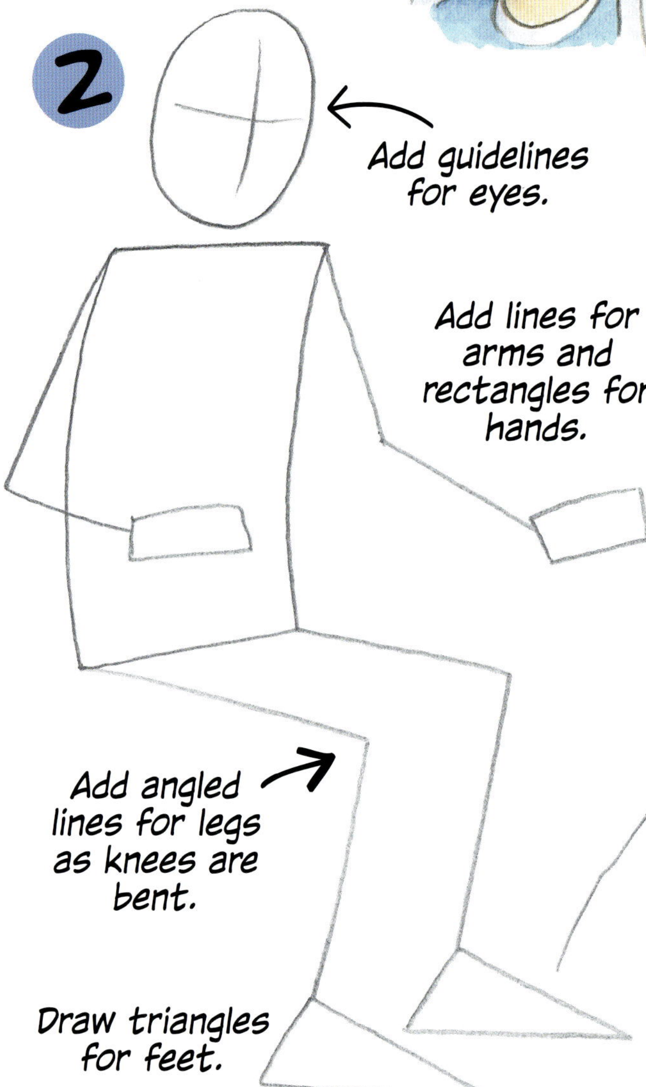

Add guidelines for eyes.

Add lines for arms and rectangles for hands.

Add angled lines for legs as knees are bent.

Draw triangles for feet.

3

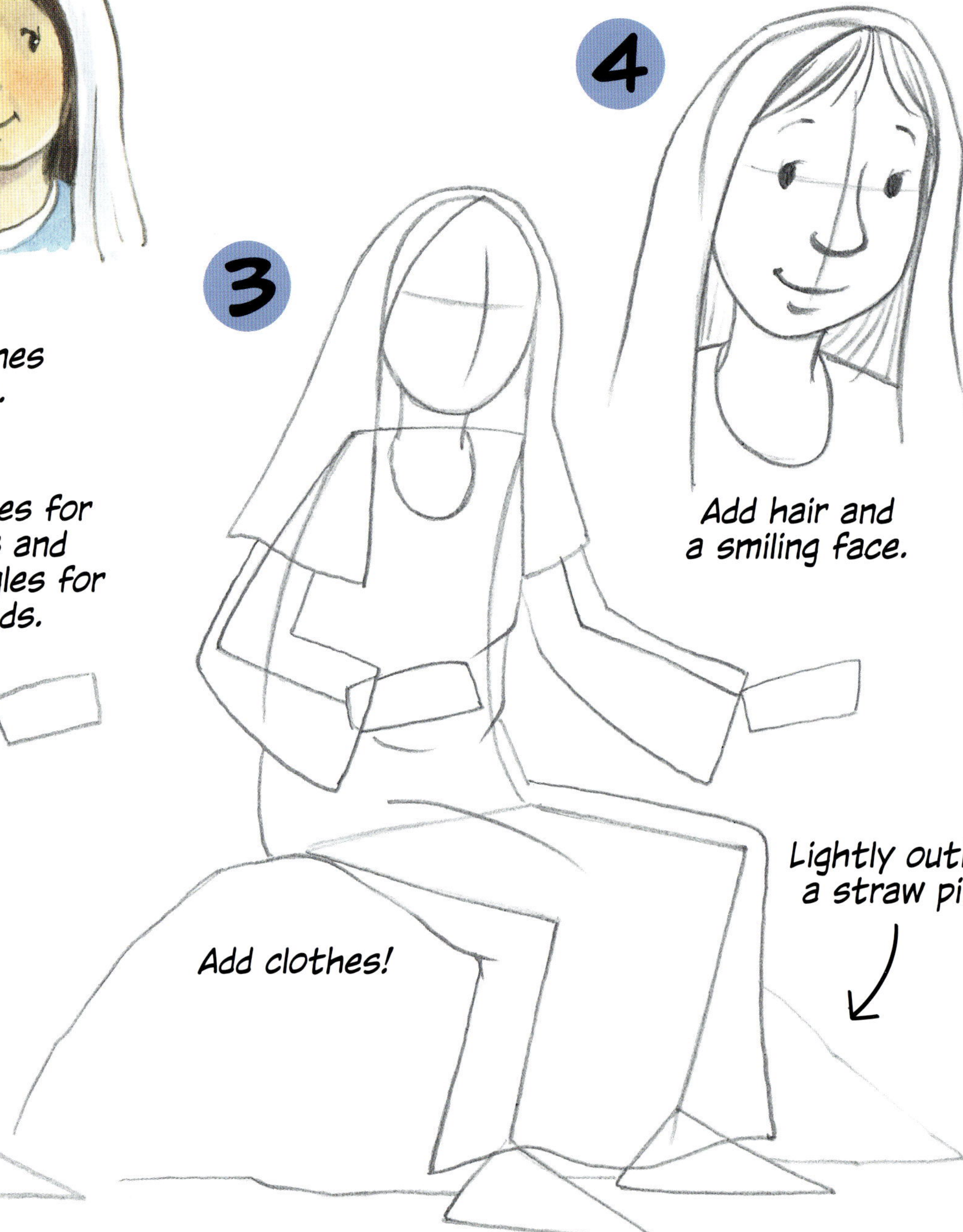

Add clothes!

Lightly outline a straw pile.

4

Add hair and a smiling face.

5 Add colour and shading.

Add thumbs and fingers to hands.

Add texture to straw.

Add toes and sandals to feet.

Draw outlines like this...

...if you want Mary to hold baby Jesus.

THE ANGEL GABRIEL

Gabriel was the messenger from God.

1

Draw an oval on top of a rectangle.

2

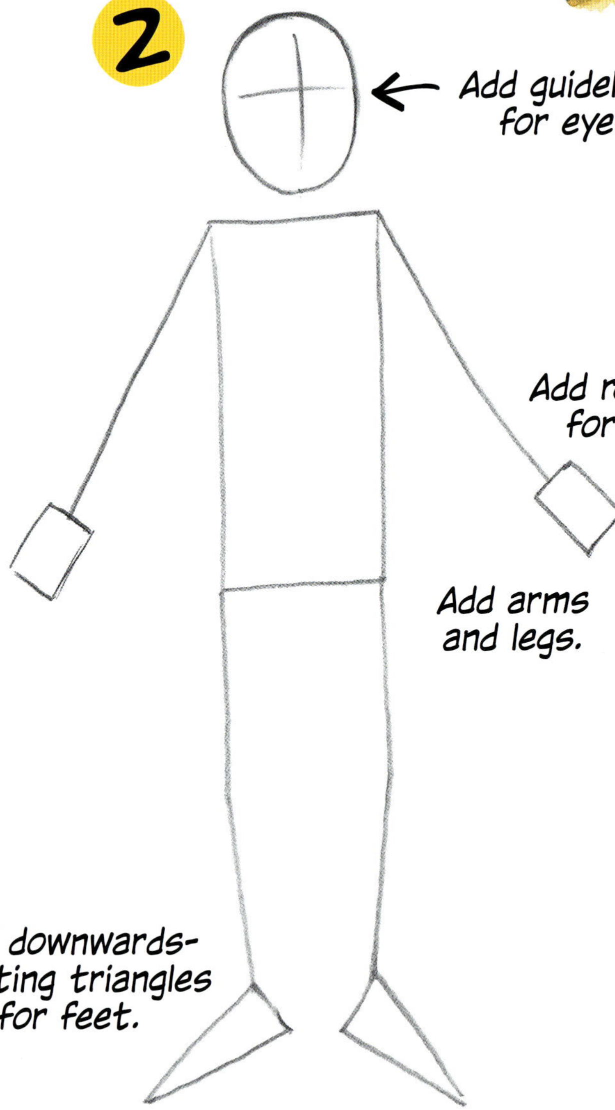

Add guidelines for eyes.

Add rectangles for hands.

Add arms and legs.

Add downwards-pointing triangles for feet.

3

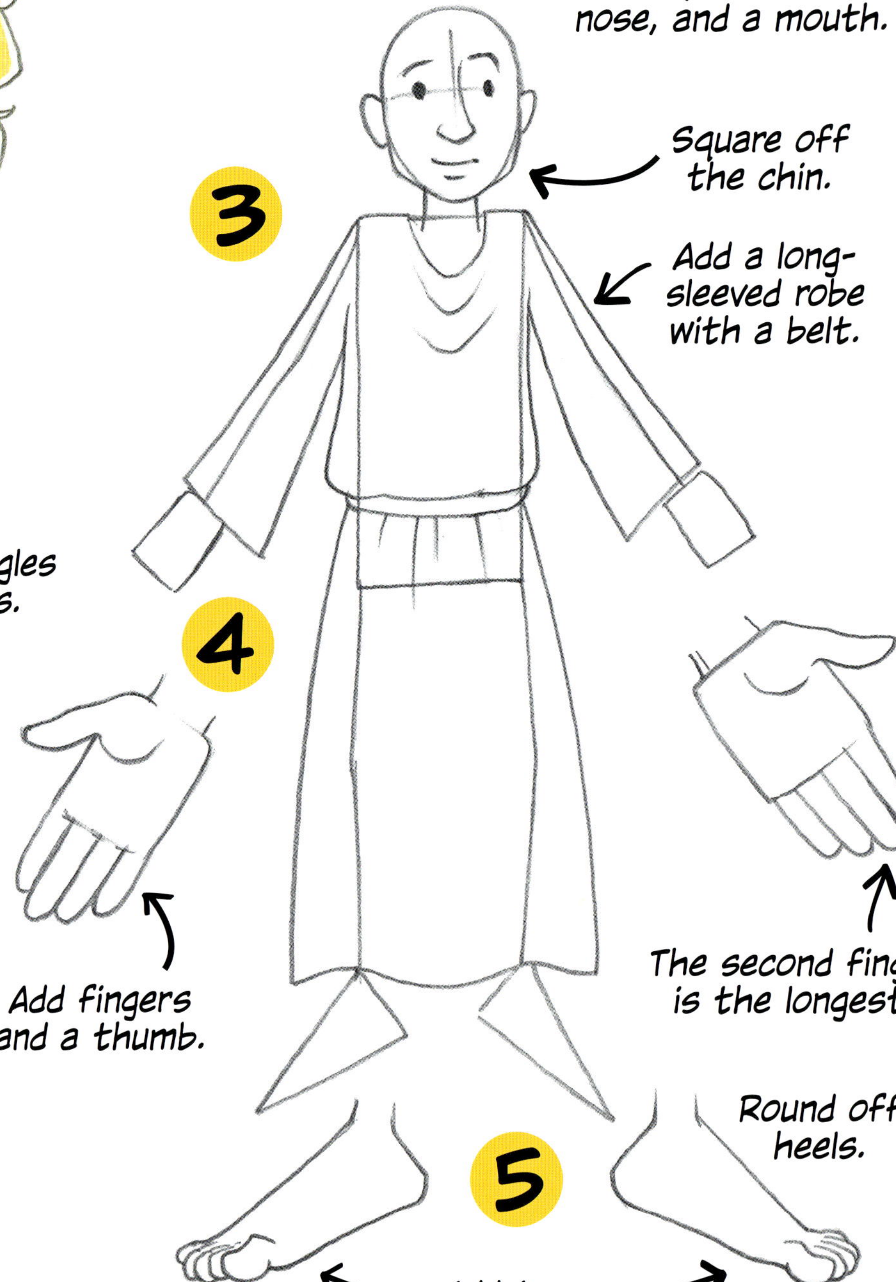

Add eyes, ears, a nose, and a mouth.

Square off the chin.

Add a long-sleeved robe with a belt.

4

Add fingers and a thumb.

The second finger is the longest!

5

Round off heels.

Add toes.

6

Draw two enormous carrot shapes on either side for the wings and use curved lines to join them to the shoulders.

7

Add lovely hair!

8

Add feather shapes on the wings in layers.

Shading on white robe can be painted in pale purpley blue.

Add long feathers at the wing tips.

Colour in white and gold.

JOSEPH

This kind carpenter married Mary.

1

Draw a circle and a slightly bent rectangle.

2

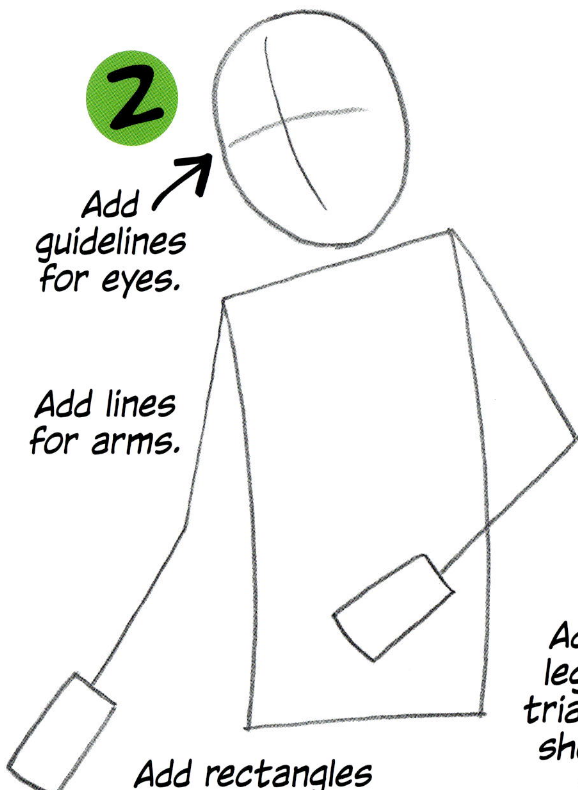

Add guidelines for eyes.

Add lines for arms.

Add rectangles for hands.

3

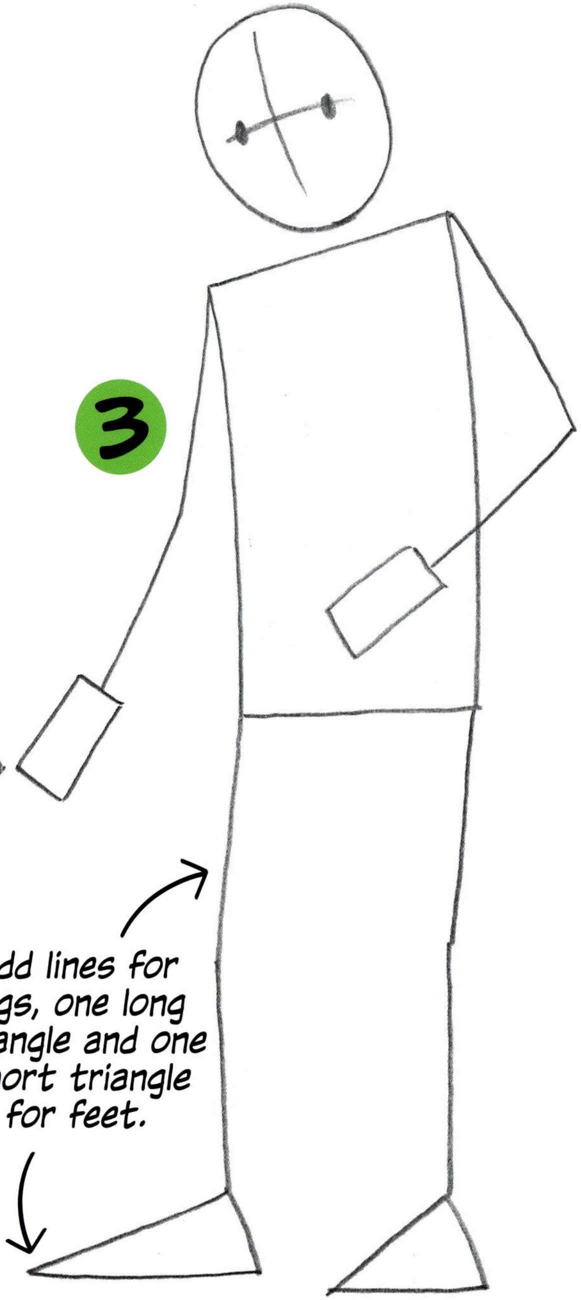

Add lines for legs, one long triangle and one short triangle for feet.

4

Add eyes, nose and a mouth.

5

Add hair and ears.

6

Add a beard.

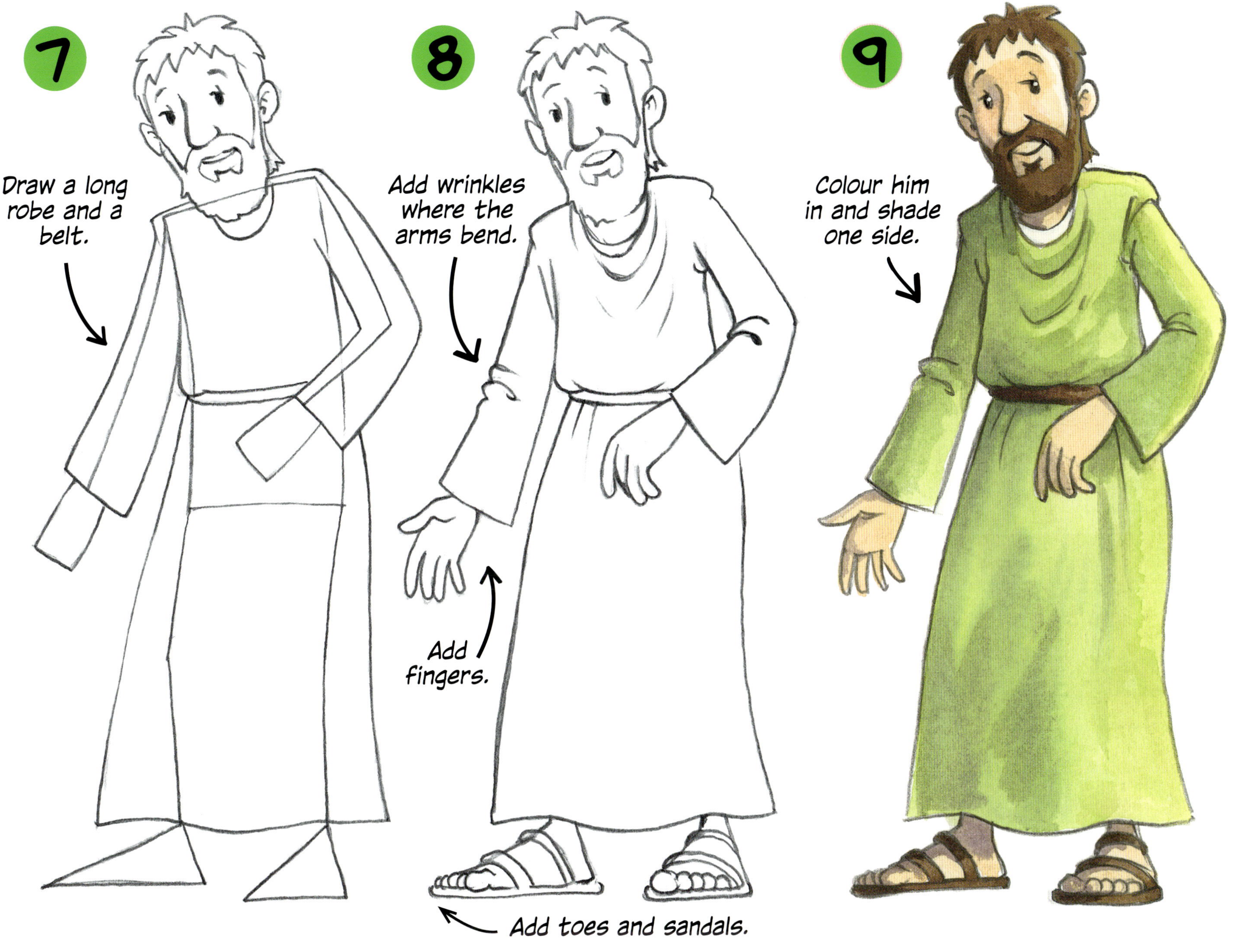
7
Draw a long robe and a belt.
8
Add wrinkles where the arms bend.
Add fingers.
Add toes and sandals.
9
Colour him in and shade one side.

DONKEY

This tired animal carried Mary all the way to Bethlehem.

1 Start with an egg shape and circle (about the same size).

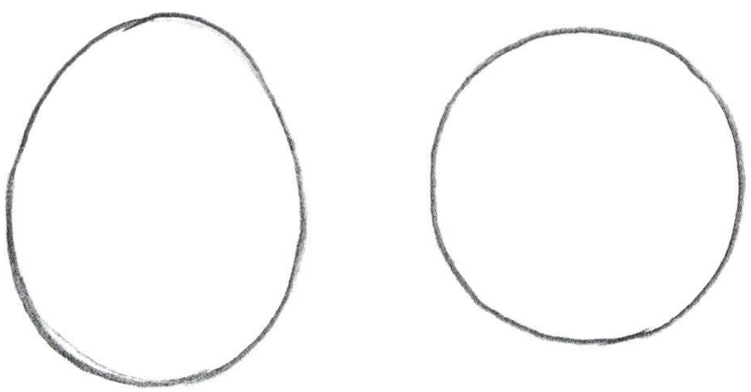

2 Join the shapes with two curved lines.

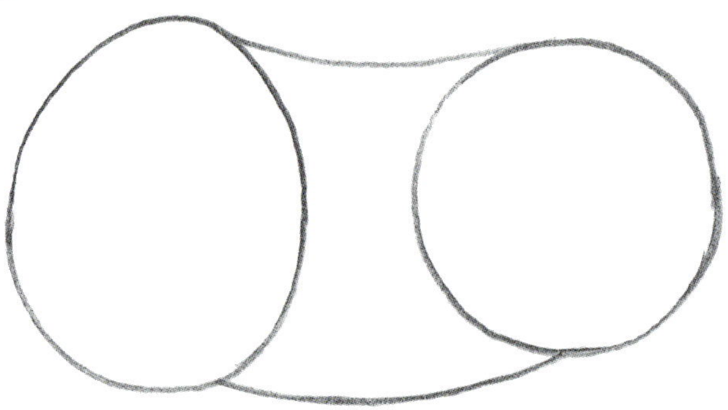

3 Add two curved lines for the neck. (They get closer together at the top end.)

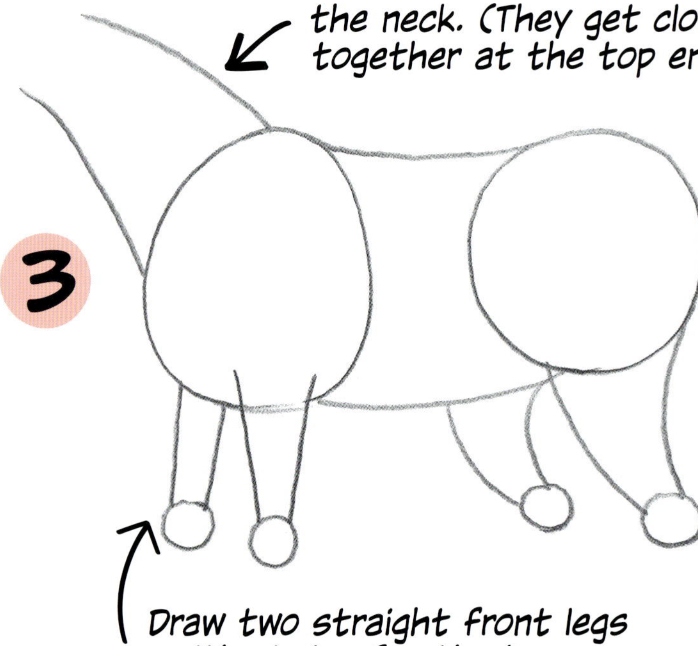

Add two back legs using curved lines and circles for knees. (They should line up with the front ones.)

Draw two straight front legs with circles for the knees.

4 Add the bottom of the legs with circles for the ankles.

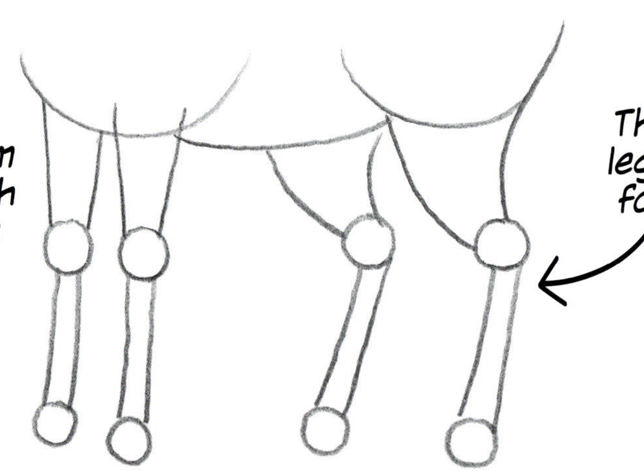

The back legs angle forward.

5 Draw a circle at the end of the neck.

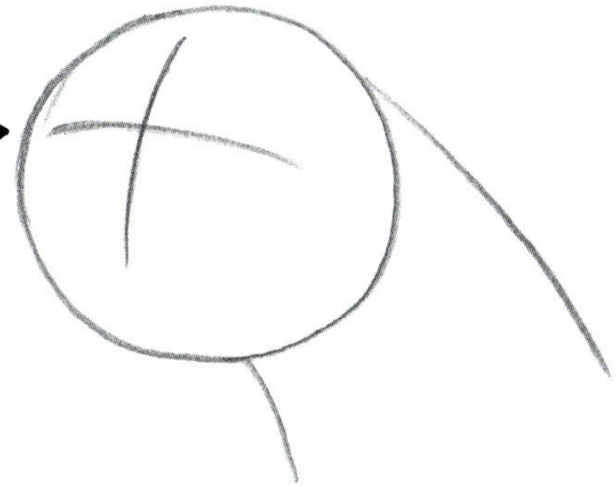

6 Add one long ear
(a bit like a bunny ear).

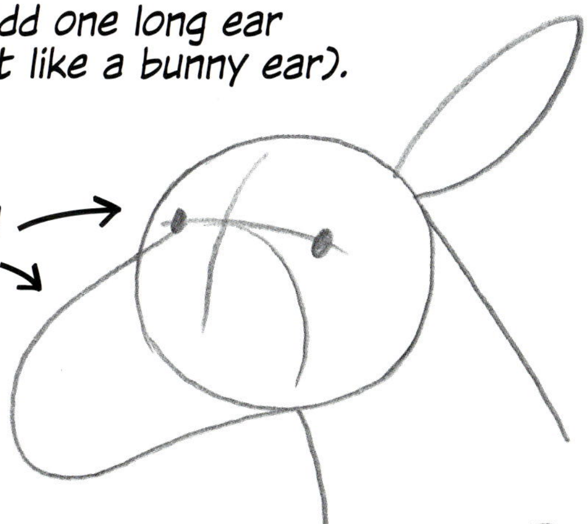

7

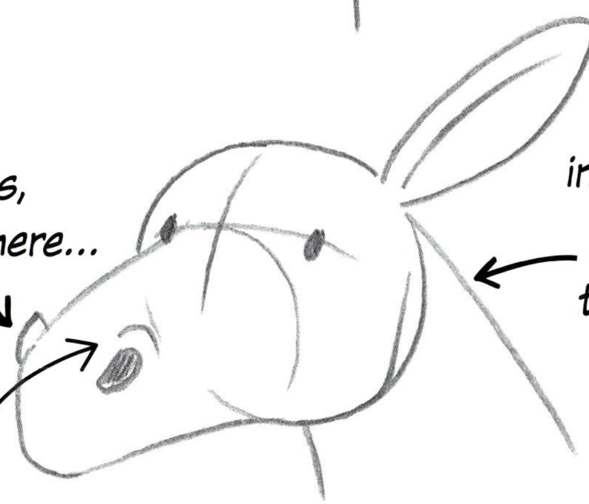

8

9 Add a tail.

10

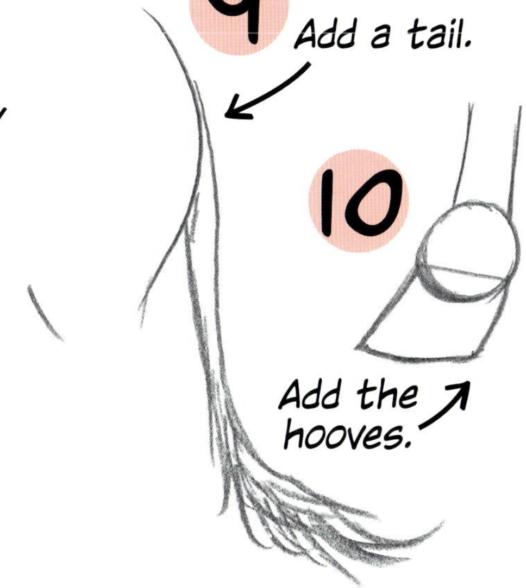

11 Colour and shade the donkey.
Make coat look a bit shaggy.

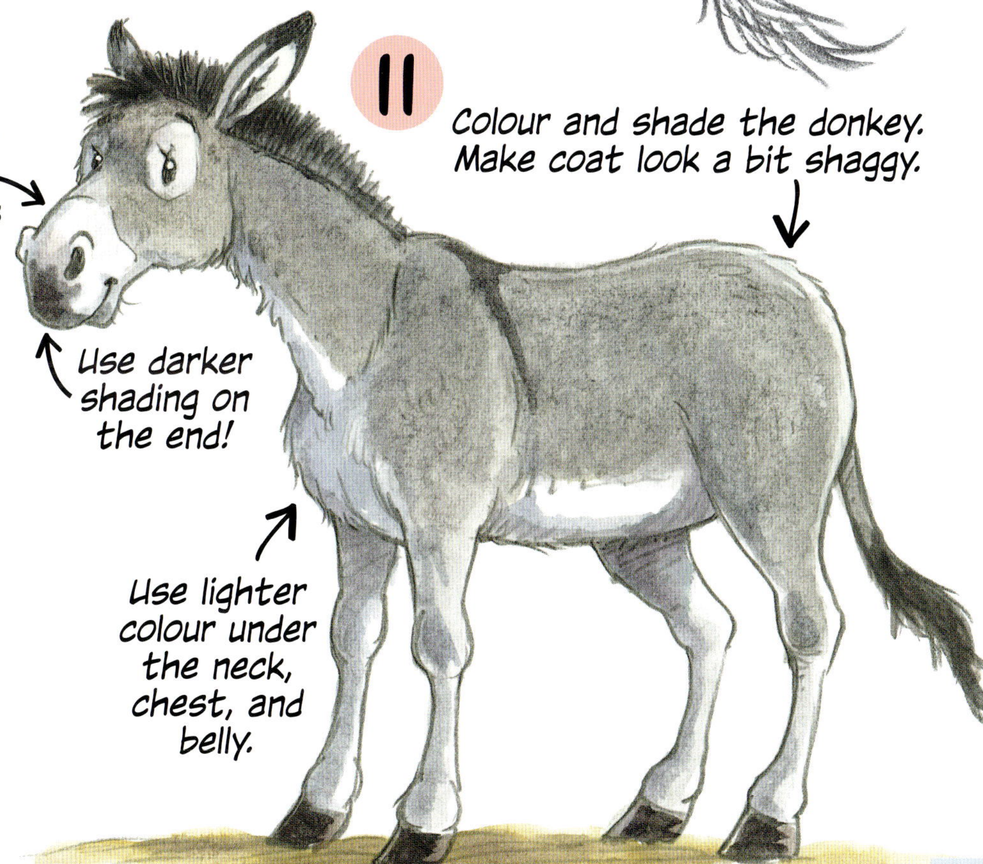

THE INNKEEPER

This busy man had an inn full of guests.

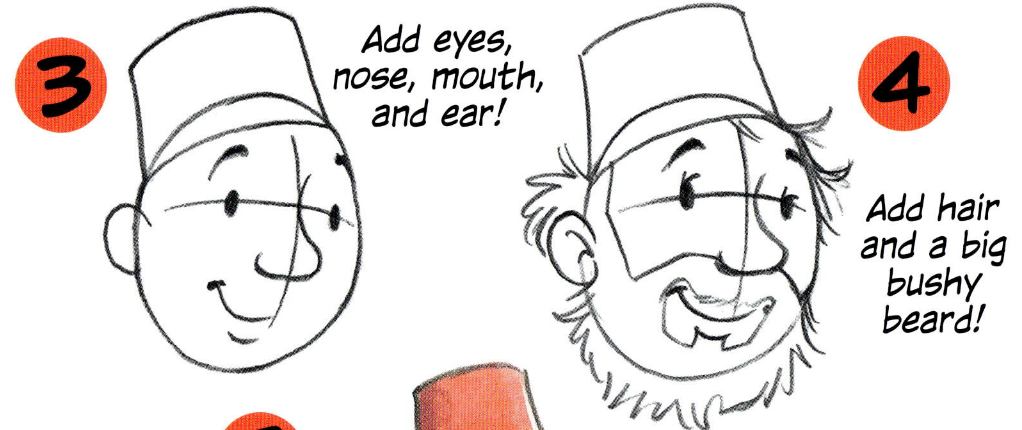

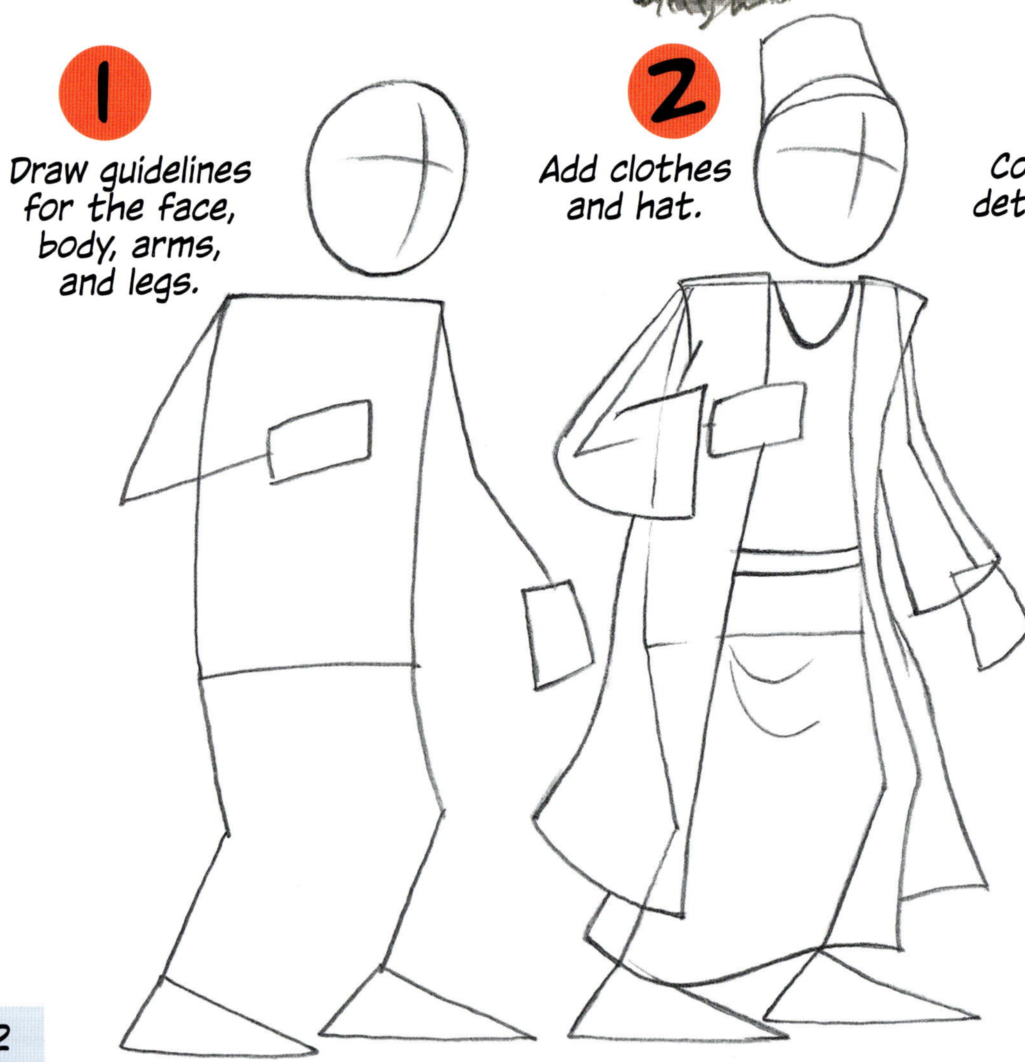

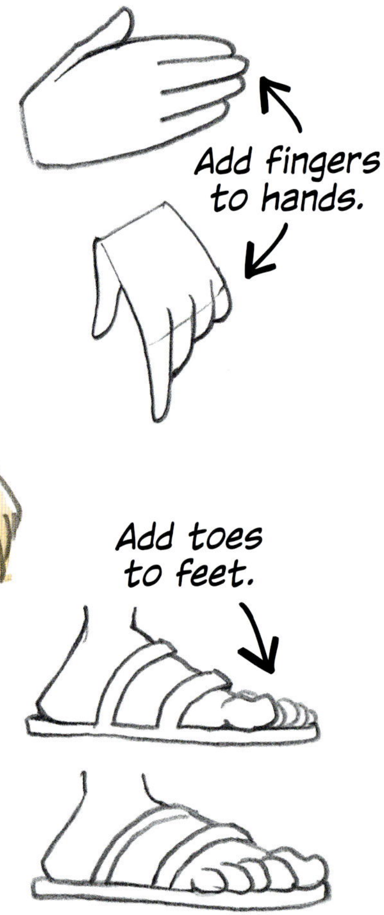

THE BABY JESUS

This new-born baby is very important.

1

Draw two circles – one for the head and one for the body.

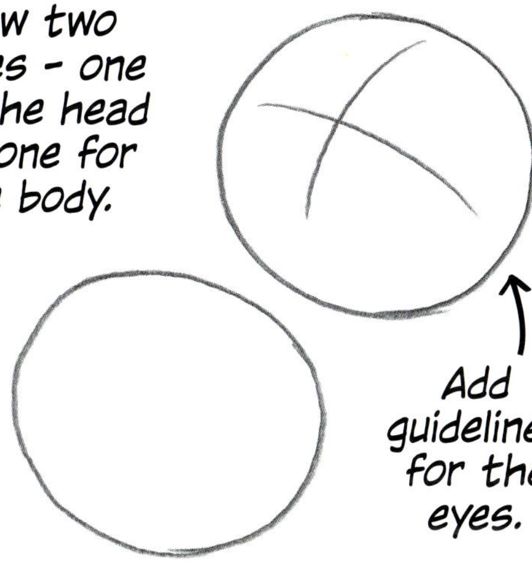

Add guidelines for the eyes.

2

Join the head and body together.

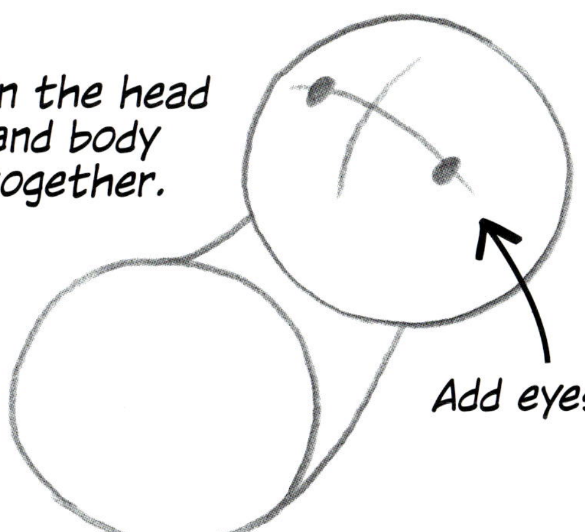

Add eyes.

3

Add a nose, eyebrows, chin, and mouth.

Add small ovals for hands and feet.

4

Add ears!

Add curved lines for arms and legs.

5

Add tiny fingers and thumbs.

Add toes and feet.

6

Add hair and turn the lower circle into clothing. Colour and shade.

You could add a piece of cloth if you like!

THE STABLE

Just draw part of the stable.
Here's what you'll need.

1 LOTS OF WOODEN BEAMS!

Draw parallel straight lines.
(Don't use a ruler - wonky is good!)

Draw two lines straight down.

Add curvy lines to look like wood grain.

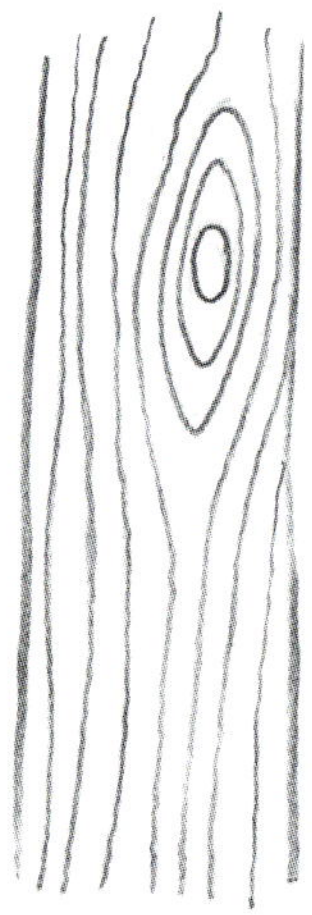

You can add circles for knot holes and draw lines curving around them.

2

Draw beams to make the rafters. Cover in straw.

3 FENCE POSTS

Draw two upright thin rectangles. (Wonky lines again!)

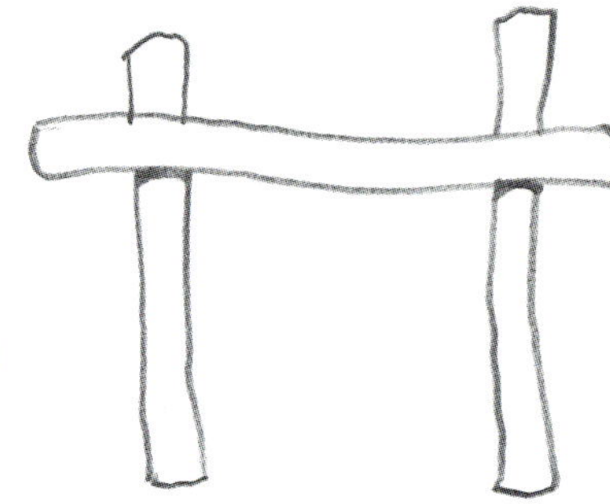

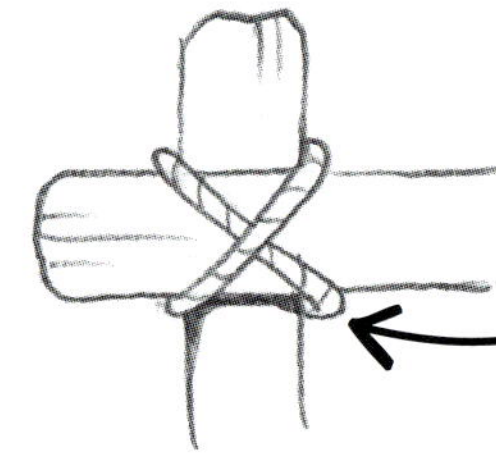

Add a horizontal rectangle in front with rounded off ends. Add x-shape for rope.

4 STRAW

Lightly sketch a heap shape.

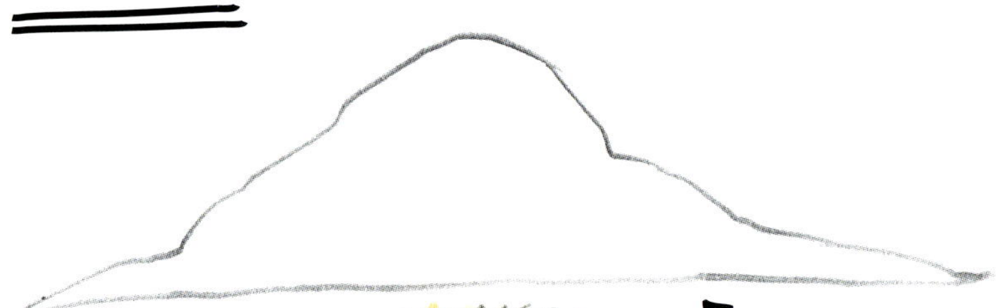

Bottom is flat.

Add random lines all around to make the pile look like straw.

*See how it all comes together on page 25!

THE MANGER

This scruffy looking box full of hay became Jesus' bed.

1

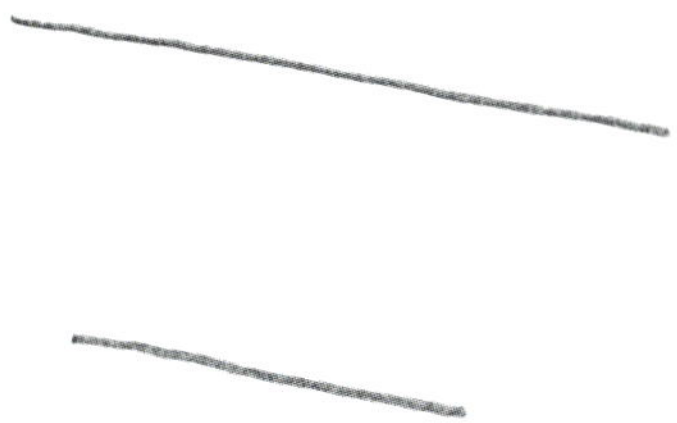

Start by drawing two angled parallel lines, with the top one longer than the bottom.

2

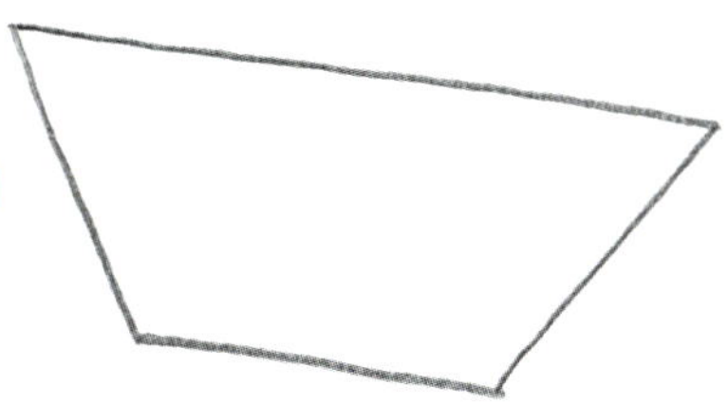

Join the ends together.

3

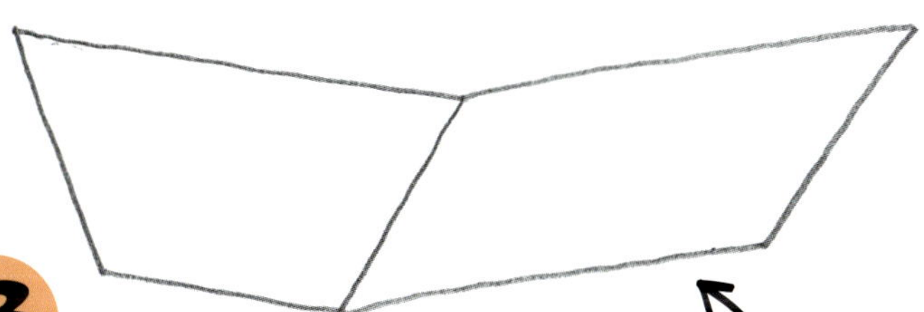

Add two more parallel lines and join them too.

4

Lightly draw a heap shape for the hay.

Add four legs at an angle.

5

Use random lines to suggest hay (see page 14).

Add shading on one side and underneath.

OXEN

Just draw the head and neck as this beast is so big.

1 Start with a circle.

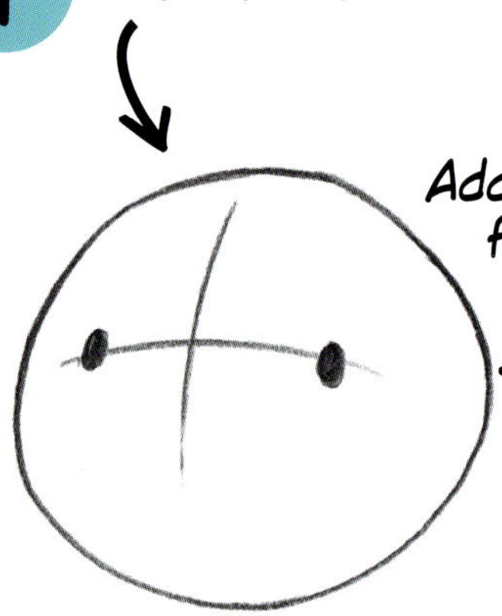

Add guidelines for eyes.

2

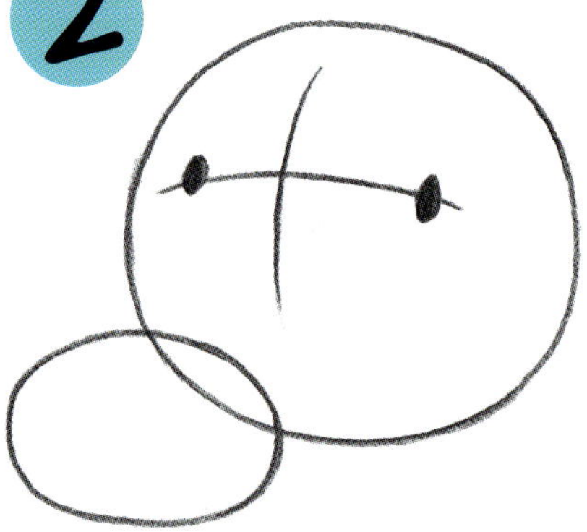

Draw an oval just overlapping the circle.

3

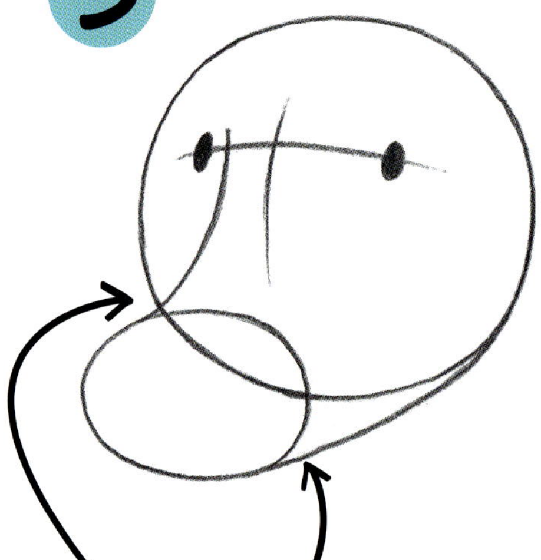

Join the oval to the circles with two curved lines.

4

Add a funky hairdo.

Draw a curved line inside the top of the oval.

Add ears.

Add a smile and a bottom lip.

Add nostrils!

5

Add horns!

Add eyelashes too if you like!

Add a neck and take it off the page or up to a wall.

Colour and shade.

GOAT

This whiskery-faced fellow could be troublesome.

1 Start with a fat bean shape.

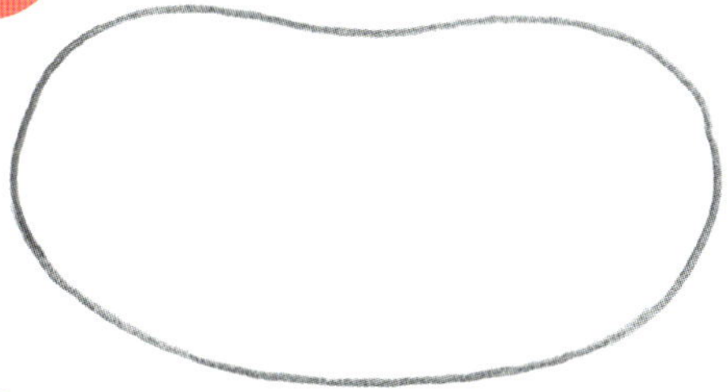

2 Add two curved lines for the neck.

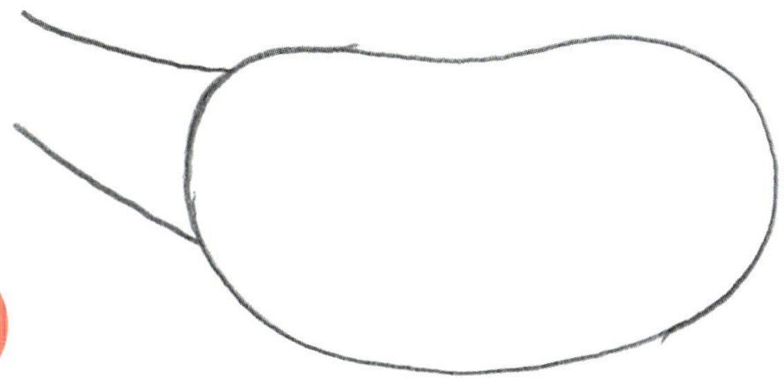

3

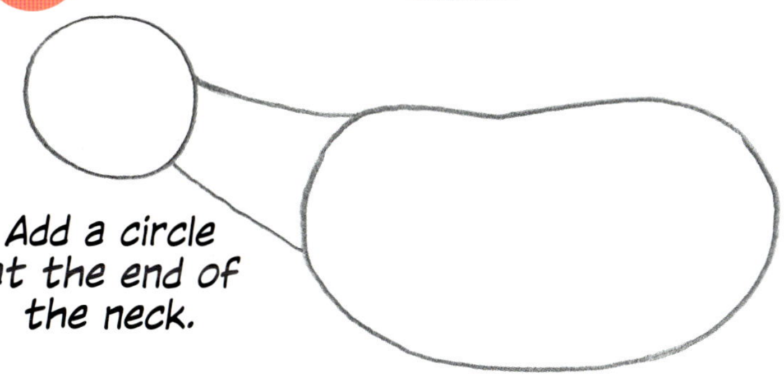

Add a circle at the end of the neck.

4 Add an ice-cream cone shape.

Add an eye.

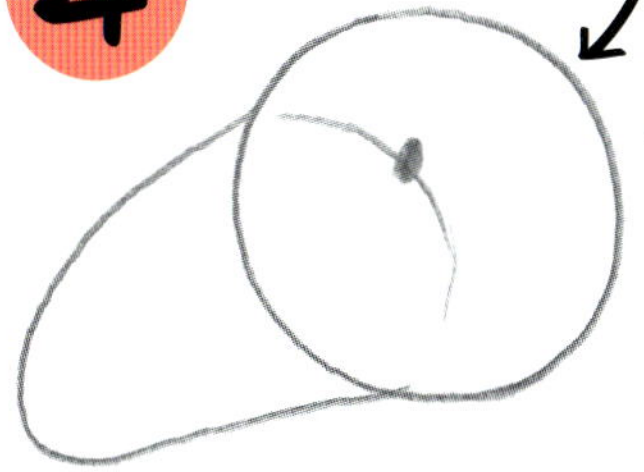

5 Add horns.

Add a floppy ear.

Add a line for a nose, a smile, and a bottom lip.

6 Draw curved lines for the back legs and circles for the knees.

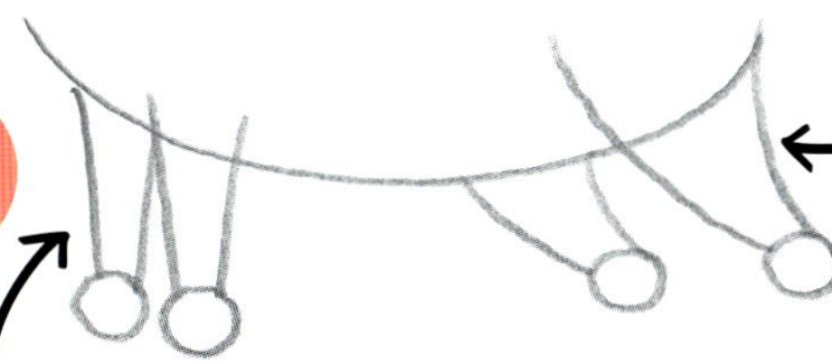

Add straight lines for the front legs and circles for the knees.

7 Add lower legs, circles for ankles, and feet.

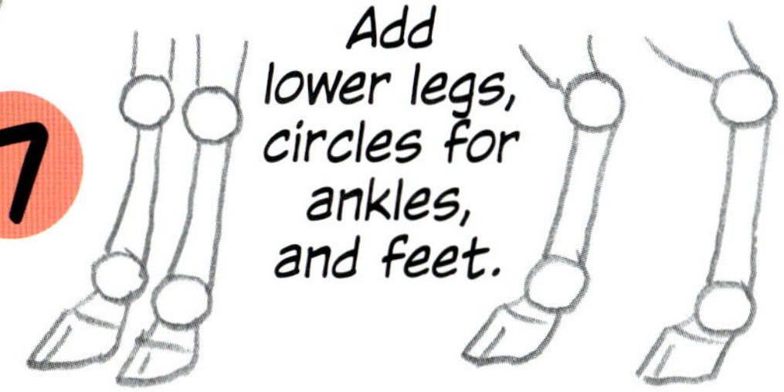

8 Add a tail.

Add a beard!

Add detail to horns and make the coat look shaggier.

Colour and shade.

OWL

Up in the rafters, a little owl looks on in wonder...

1

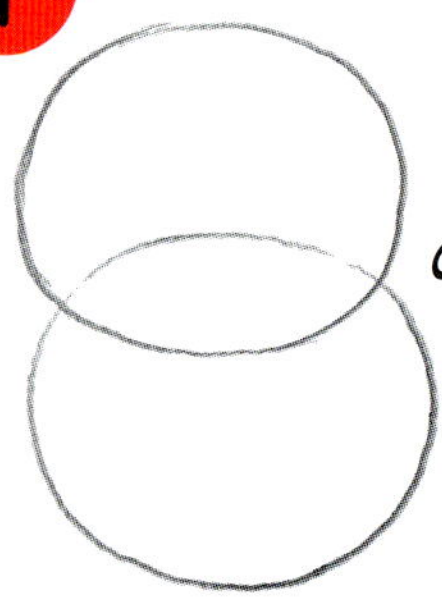

Draw two overlapping circles.

2

Draw a heart shape on the face.

3

Add eyes, a carrot-shaped beak, and a leaf-shaped wing.

4

Add a bump for the other wing.

Add arrows for chest feathers and sausage shapes for toes.

5

Colour and shade.

DOG

This visitor is very excited!

1

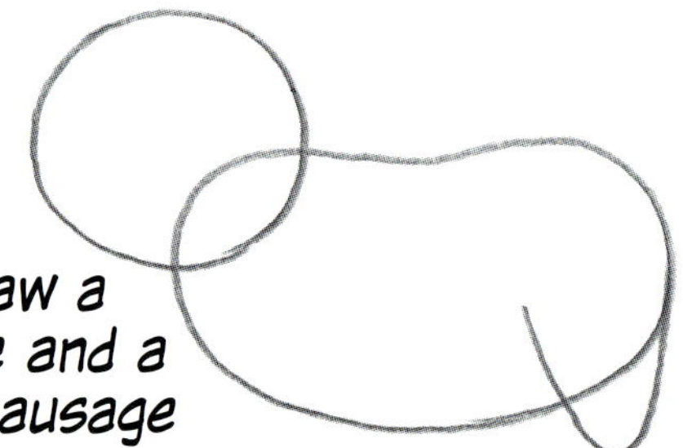

Draw a circle and a fat sausage shape.

Add a rounded 'V' shape at the back.

2

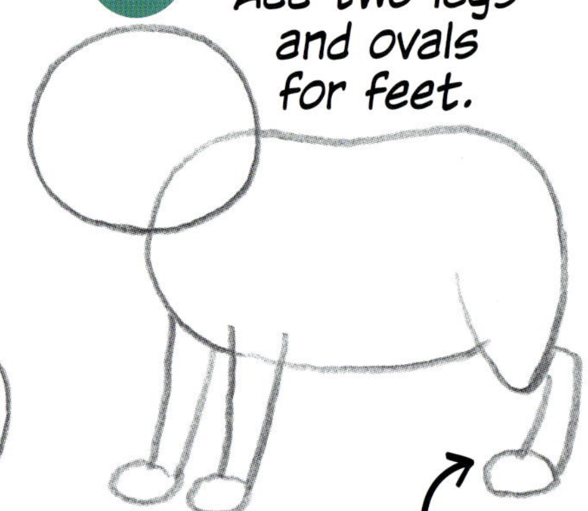

Add two legs and ovals for feet.

Add back leg behind the 'V'.

3

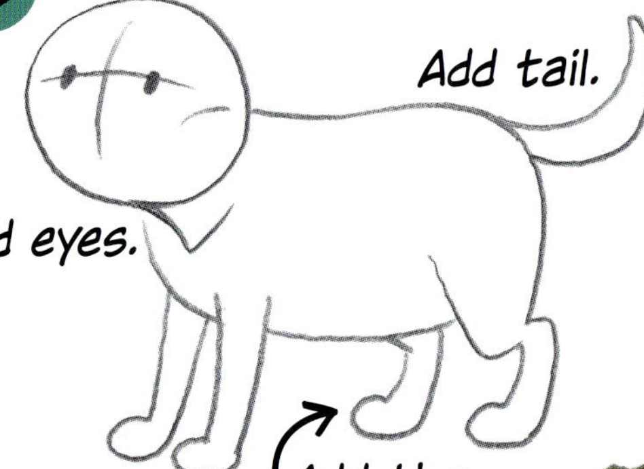

Add eyes.

Add tail.

Add the last leg.

4

Add semi-circles for ears.

Draw a beaker-shaped muzzle and an oval-shaped nose.

5

Add a smile and details to feet, and colour!

Use lines to make his tail wag!

CHICKENS

Sssh! Stop clucking, chickens!

1 Start with a cup shape.

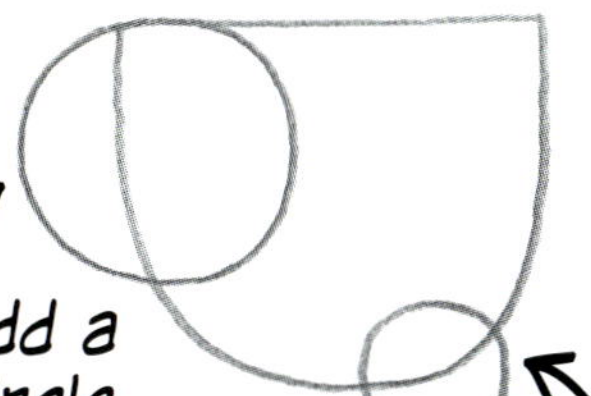

Add a circle here.

Add a little circle here.

2 Add a neck and a circle for the head.

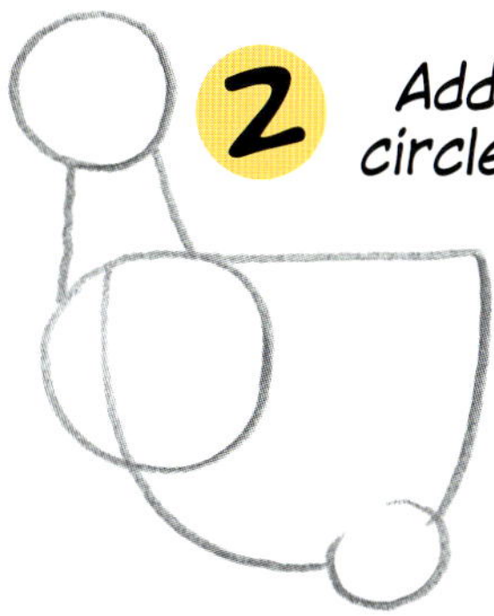

3 Add a tail.

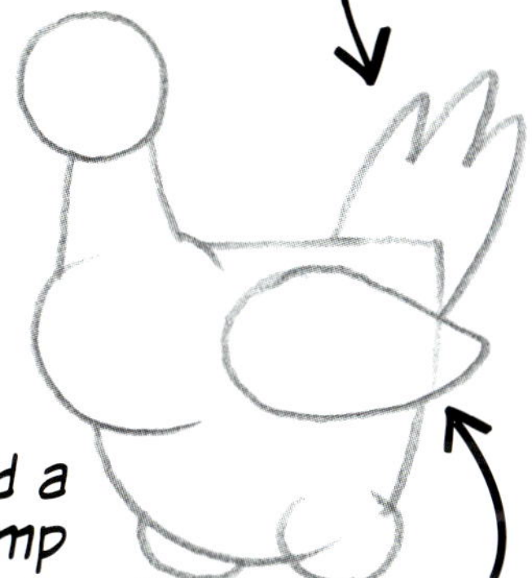

Add a bump here.

Add a leaf-shaped wing.

4

Add eyes.

Add a triangular beak.

Add feather detail.

Add two feet.

5

Draw a crest, wattles, and a smile!

6

Add colour and shading.

RABBIT

Hop along in...

1

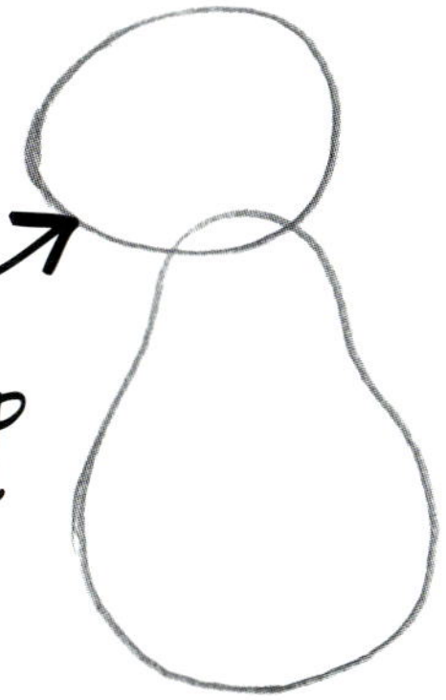

Draw an egg on top of a pear.

2

Add ears.

Add eyes.

Draw a 'Y' shape for the mouth and nose.

Draw a curved line for the legs.

Add feet.

3

Draw two ovals for the paws.

Add a curved line for the arm.

Add lines for the fingers and toes.

4

Add fur, whiskers, and a tail!

Then colour and shade.

AND A MOUSE!

1

Draw a fat carrot on a pear shape.

2

Add nose, ears, eye, and tail.

3 Add whiskers, hands, and feet.

And colour!

BETHLEHEM HOUSES

Start with box-shapes and draw a town.

1 Start by drawing a rectangle.

2 Add two short lines: one going slightly down at the top and one going slightly upwards at the bottom.

3

Then join the lines together with another vertical line.

4

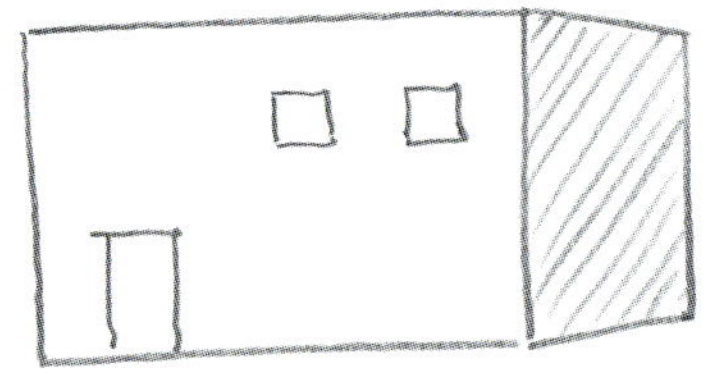

Shade the side and add square windows and a door.

5 Shade the inside of the doors and windows leaving a strip to the left.

Add angled shadow top left.

6 Try different shaped buildings, all with flat roofs.

Add different doors and windows.

7 Some buildings have a shallow dome on top.

8

Draw a group of houses together and add some trees.

ROMAN SOLDIER

Don't get on the wrong side of these grumpy soldiers.

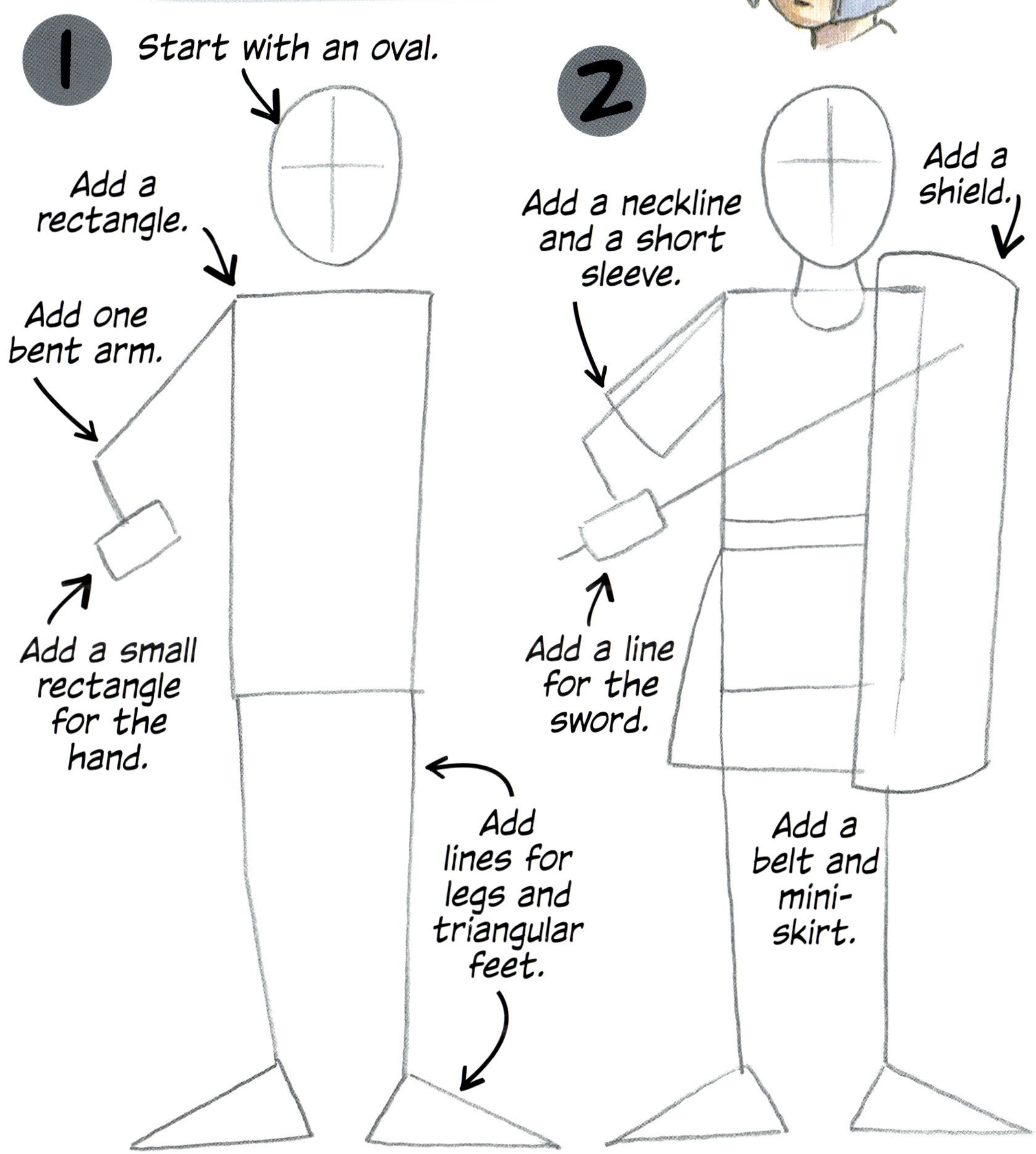

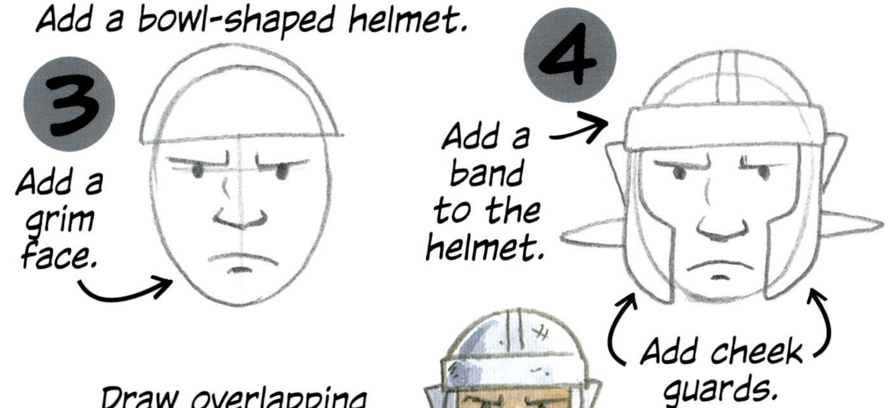

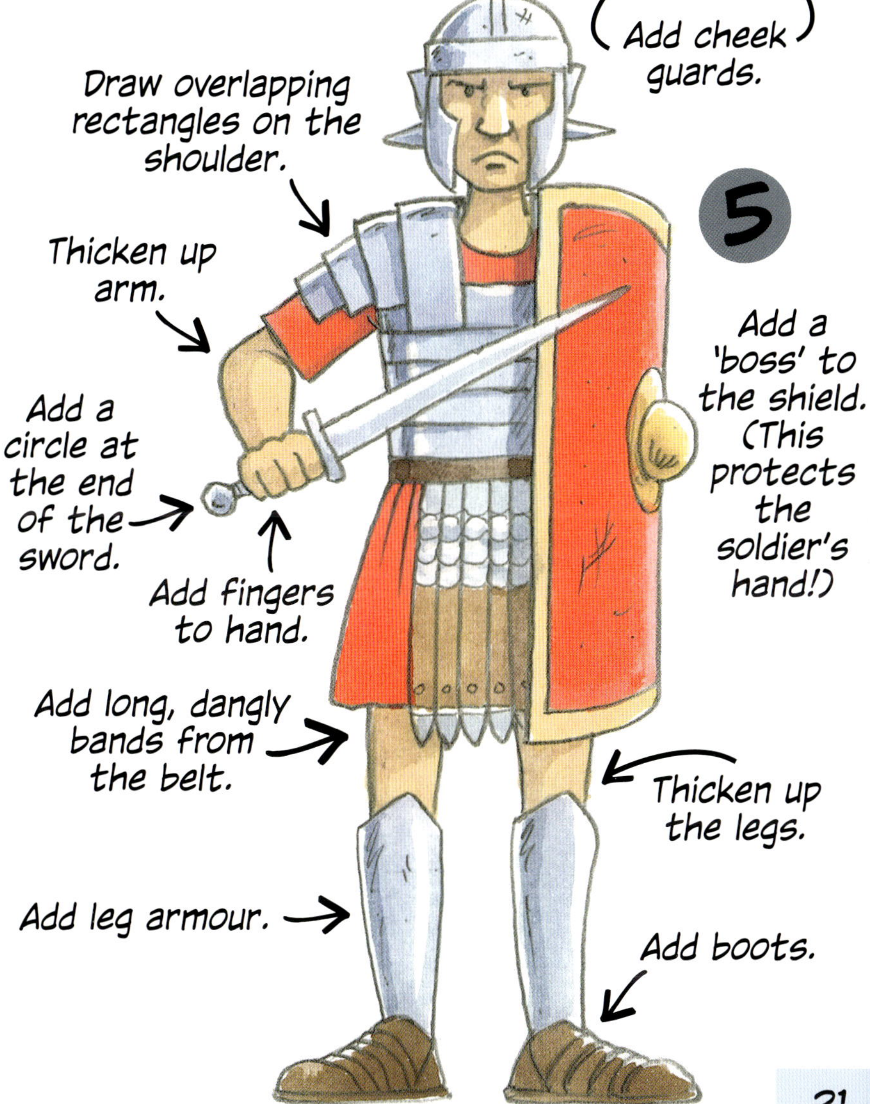

SHEPHERDS

These fellows are so excited to visit baby Jesus.

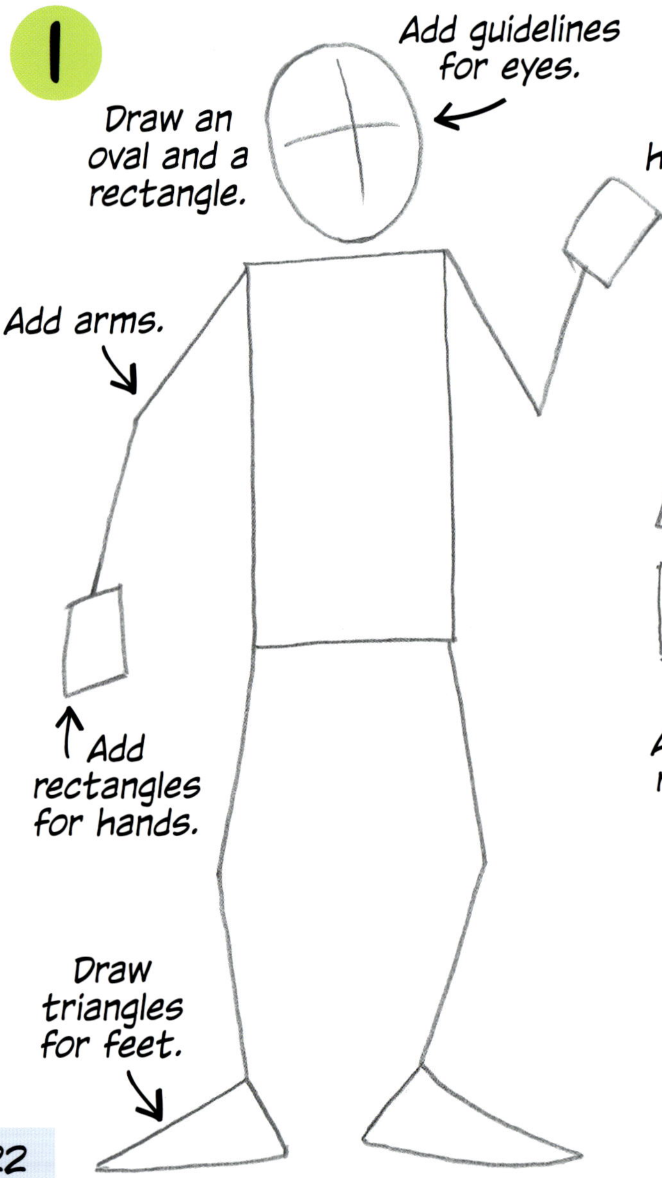

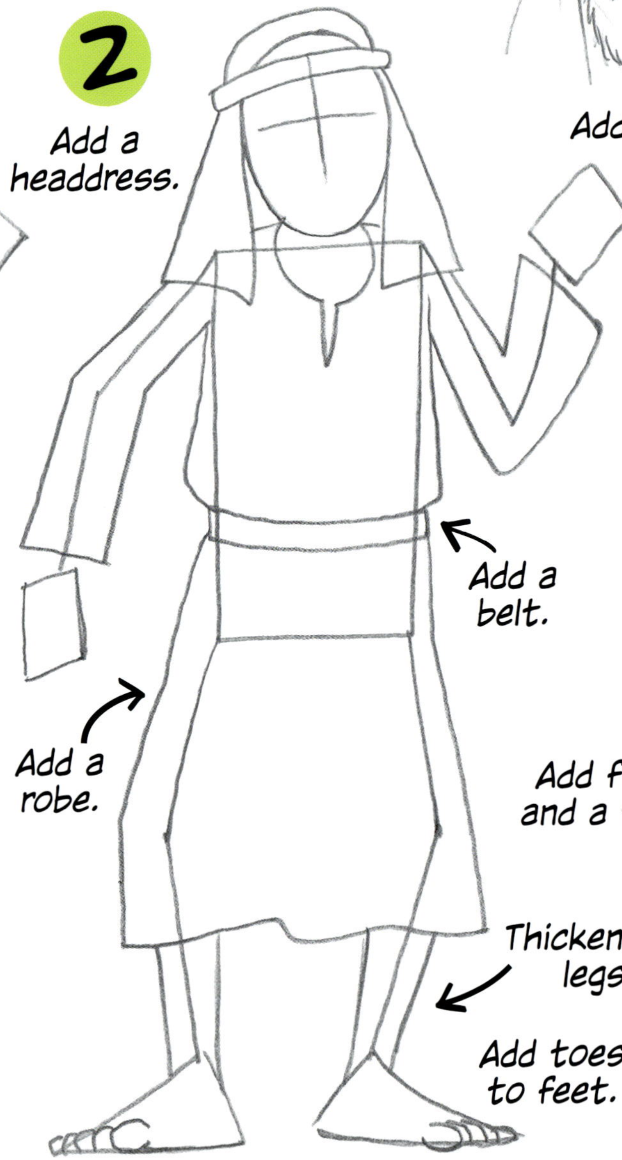

THERE WERE LOTS OF SHEPHERDS AND ANGELS!

Try different expressions, hair styles, and beards.

Try using different body shapes and positions for different characters.

The guidelines show which way he's looking.

Try different clothes, too.

SHEEP AND LAMB

These woolly animals want to visit, too.

1

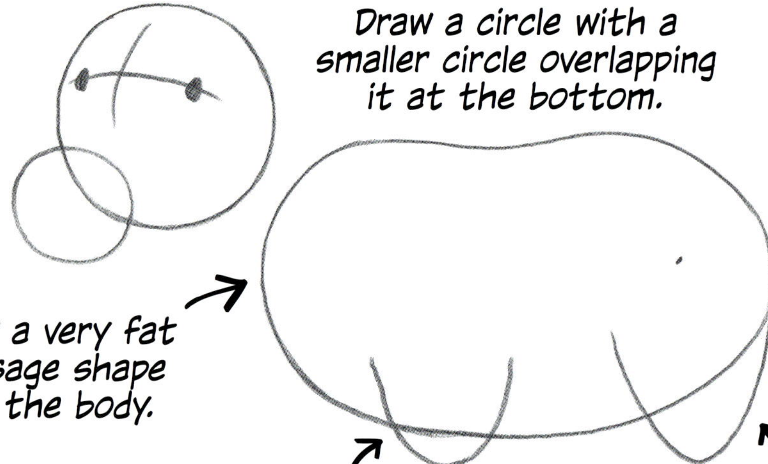

Draw a circle with a smaller circle overlapping it at the bottom.

Draw a very fat sausage shape for the body.

Draw two rounded 'V' shapes.

2

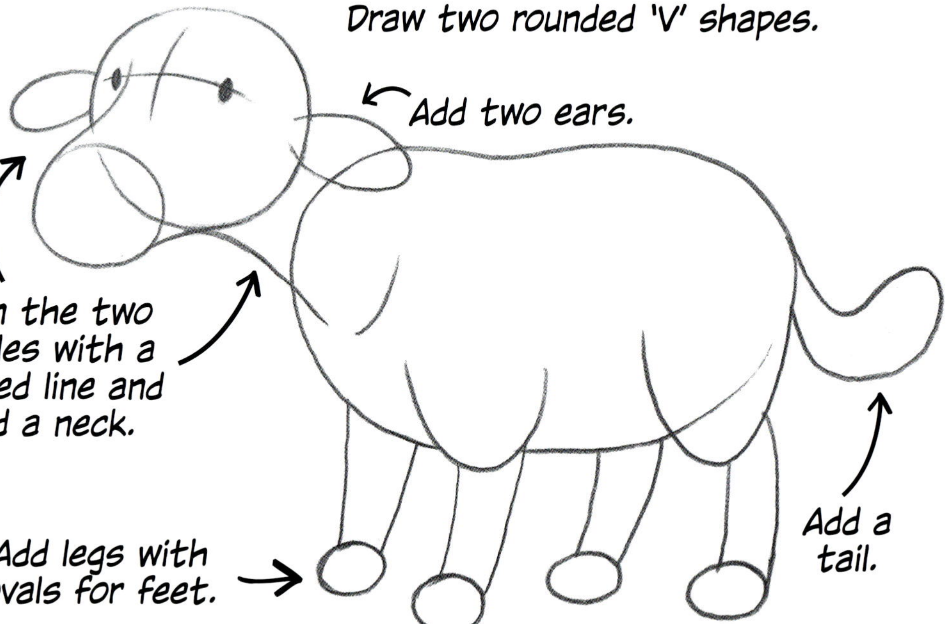

Add two ears.

Join the two circles with a curved line and add a neck.

Add a tail.

Add legs with ovals for feet.

3

Add woolly texture and a nice hairdo!

Add a 'Y' for the nose and a smile.

Add hooves to feet.

Lambs are smaller and have shorter noses and bigger ears.

Also, start with a thinner sausage shape.

An open mouth makes the lamb look more excited!

THREE WISE MEN

These stargazers brought gifts for Jesus.

1

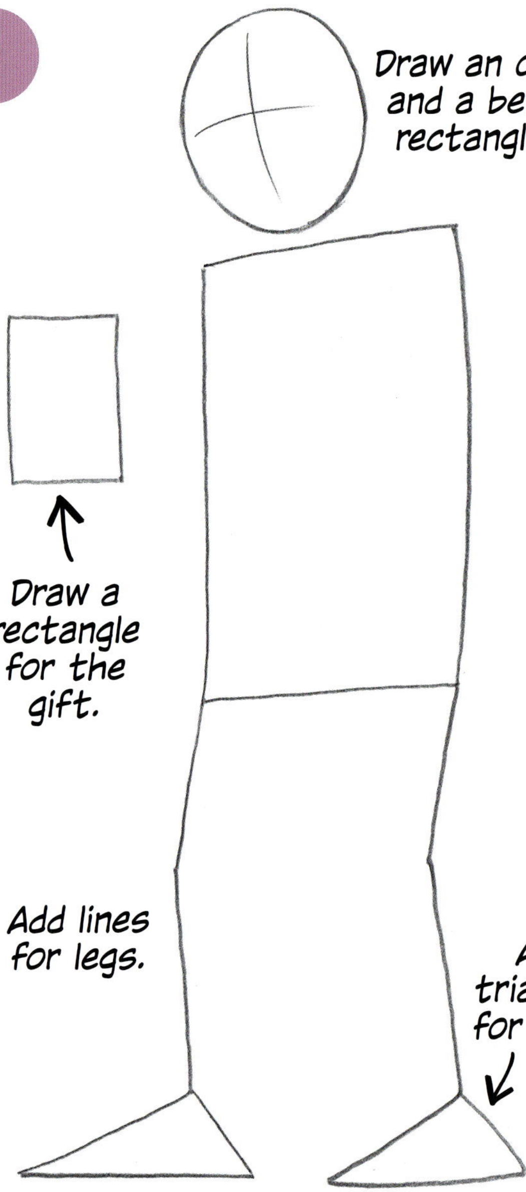

Draw an oval and a bent rectangle.

Draw a rectangle for the gift.

Add lines for legs.

Add triangles for feet.

2

Add a face.

Draw rectangles for hands on the gift then add lines back to the shoulders for the arms. (It's easier this way.)

3 Add details to the gift.

Add fingers to hands.

4

Add a long robe.

Round off triangles to look more like shoes.

5

Make each wise man look unique with different faces, hats, and beards.

6

Try changing the body shape a little.

7

Draw different outfits for each wise man.

Add a cape.

CAMEL

This grumpy beast has a hump.

1

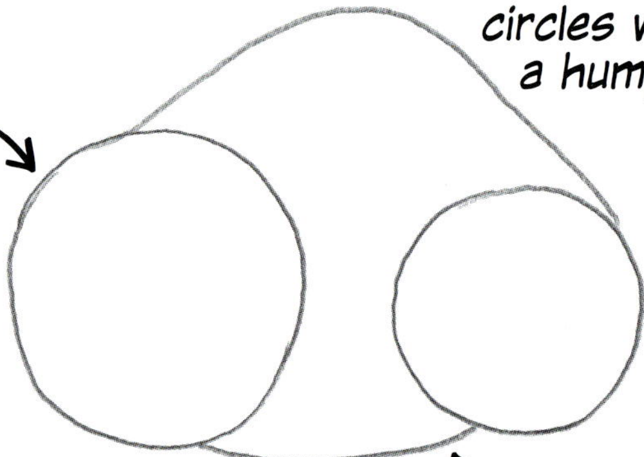

Draw two circles, one slightly bigger than the other.

Join the circles with a hump.

Add a curved line.

2

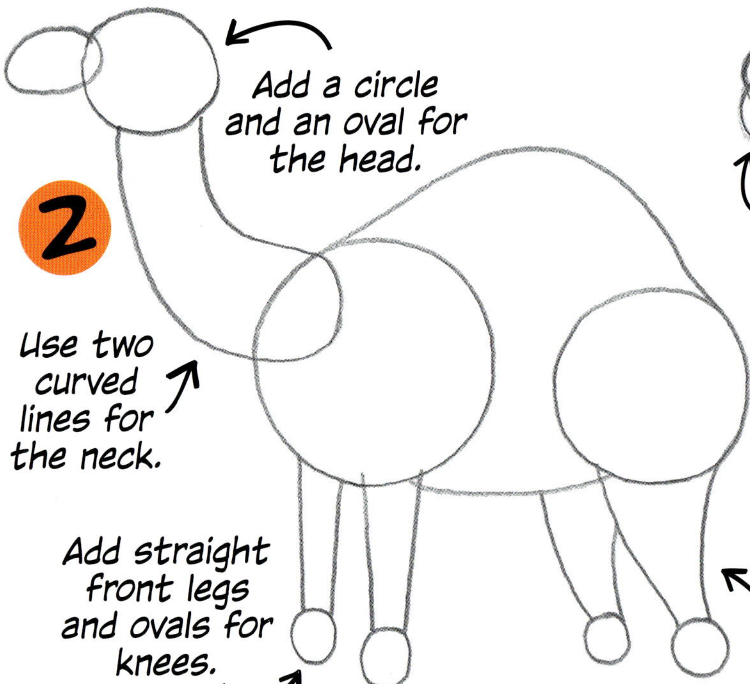

Add a circle and an oval for the head.

Use two curved lines for the neck.

Add straight front legs and ovals for knees.

Back legs are curved.

3

Add one ear.

Add a nostril and a grumpy mouth.

Add a closed eye.

Add shaggy fur.

4

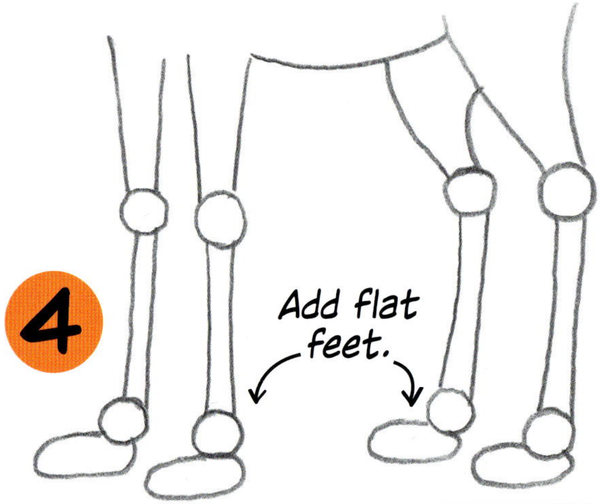

Add flat feet.

Add the bottom half of the legs.

5

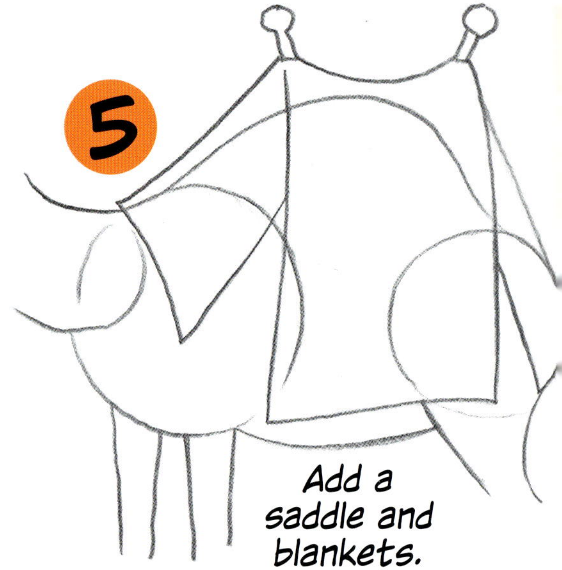

Add a saddle and blankets.

6

Colour a pattern on the blankets.

Add a bell and reins.

Add a tail.

JESUS THE TODDLER

When Jesus was about two years old he had a visit from three wise men.

1

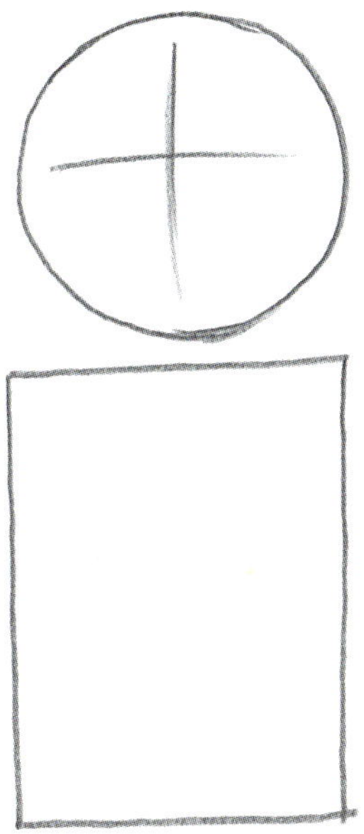

Add guidelines for eyes.

Draw a circle with a small rectangle underneath.

(Small children have big heads and small bodies.)

2

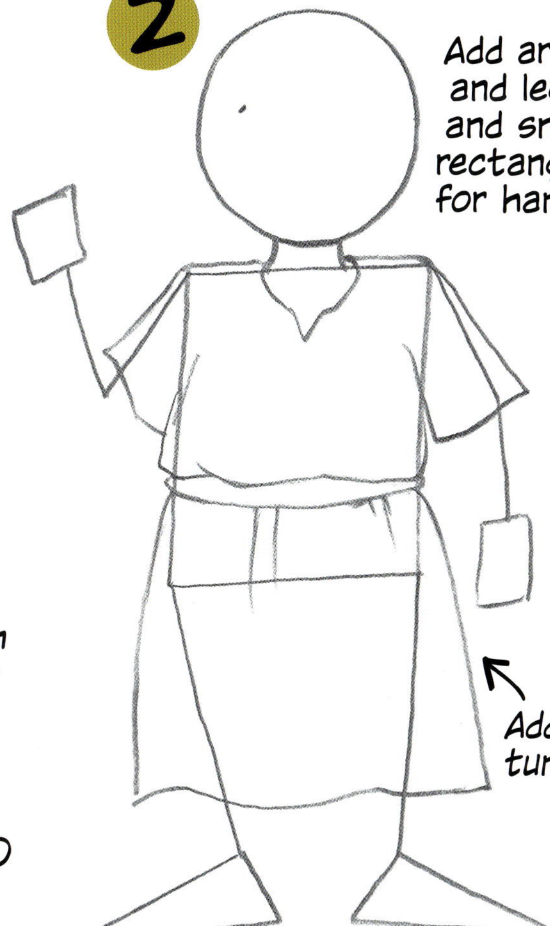

Add arms and legs, and small rectangles for hands.

Add a tunic.

Add small triangles for the feet.

3

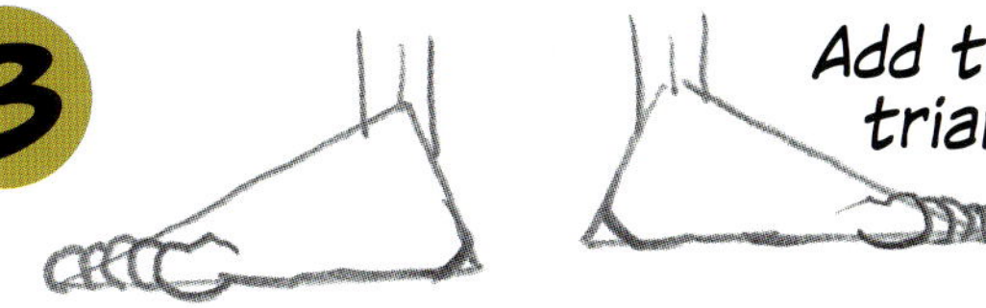

Add toes to the triangle feet.

Round off the corners.

4

Add fingers and thumbs.

Each finger gets shorter.

5

Add facial details, ears, and long hair.

6

Movement lines make Jesus wave!

Add shading and detail on the clothes.

KING HEROD

He's mad, bad, and very angry.

3 Round off the edges of the rectangles.

Draw four folded fingers.

Draw a bent thumb.

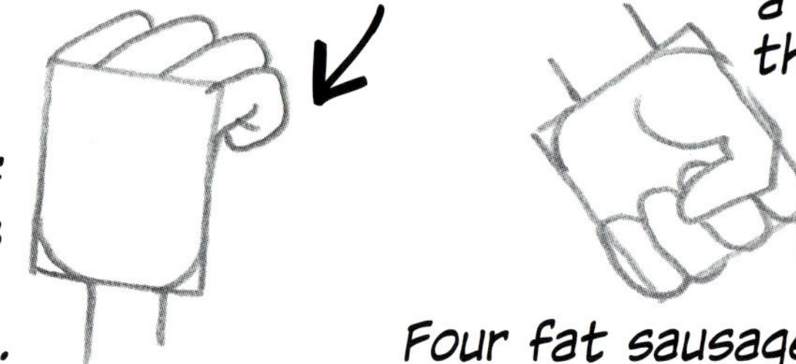

Four fat sausage shapes tucked under the thumb.

1 Start with an oval for the head and a rectangle for the body.

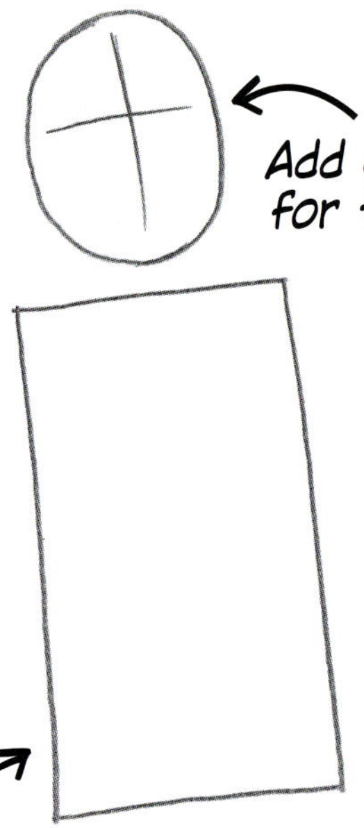

Add guidelines for the eyes.

The body is at a bit of an angle.

2 Add arms; one up, one down, and legs with bent knees.

Draw rectangles for hands.

Add triangles for feet.

4 Add clothes – a long robe over a belted tunic.

Use curving lines to show movement.

5

Draw a crown on his head with spikes on the top.

Add ears.

Add eyes and a pointy nose.

6

Add angry, slanted eyebrows and a mouth like a bent fishfinger.

7

Draw angry lines on forehead.

Add mad hair.

Add a pointy beard.

8

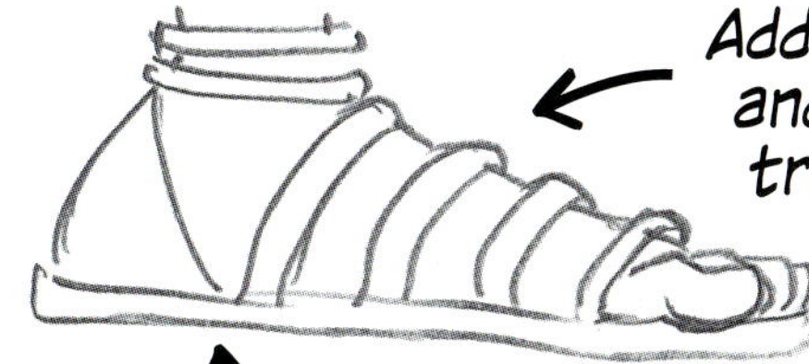

Add curved straps and toes to the triangular feet.

Add soles to the shoes.

9

Colour his face red.

Add creases to the arms.

Add movement lines.